RONDEAUX

RONDEAUX

□□□□□□□□□□□□

Laura Moriarty

ROOF

Some of these works were originally published in *Talisman*, *How(ever)*, *Conjunctions, Temblor, Hambone, o.blek, Ottotole, Boundary 2*, and *The Best American Poetry 1990*.

ISBN: 0-937804-39-8
Library of Congress Catalog Card No.: 90-061555

Design and cover by Susan Bee.
Book production by Deborah Thomas.
Cover: Detail of *Salome* by Gustave Moreau.
Author photo by Norma Cole.
Special thanks to Jerry Estrin for his help in the production of this book.

This book was made possible, in part, by grants from the National Endowment for the Arts and the New York State Council on the Arts.

ROOF BOOKS
are published by
The Segue Foundation
303 East 8th St.
New York, New York 10009

Contents

Each page a day
Each rectangle outlined
On the sky there is movement
We are under it it is raining
These days remembering back
To that day actually the present
Streets meeting already writing
As if divided I write you and see
Each page handing it over directly
You at the same time in a speech
Make writing into life
Paper in hair and eyes
Mixed with the general storm
Inundated with each other
Each page says anything

Naked still on the second day
A current goes through my handwriting
My diary overcome the sea
Is like silk today There is
An unusual situation with us and the sun
And the moon big on the horizon
This is the story of the birth of Diana
Of your creation of a lover on paper
Naked but keeping track I write
To wish the season upon you
From the middle of my life to the middle of yours
In this rude outdoor existence exposed
Writing that I realized I missed the floods
As they pulled away revealing only mud long covered
Naked at last again as I write this

As I taste it's warm almost hot
If quiet I can hear as well as see
A woman chopping celery in a bright
Kitchen from the back window
But she doesn't see me watching
Her movements are precise and quickly
She has everything laid out One must
Learn how to cook or how to drink tea
As I taste as if I were made
Only of the ability to taste
As if I were taught to stop with tea
And to wait to turn on the lights
By one whose experience retains heat
Like a day that was warm or a cup
As I taste it seems to stay hot

Aye, rarely said But you have said
When long When days have gone on
A week spent and leaning against
Some booth or bar say Aye and stop
Not for yes or always though yes always
You put a word to a long even
Breath I have heard you say
With some awe at the slowness of time
Aye, rarely said But you so often
Offer this equivalent for sighing
Named for a vote or forever
Each day a law that passes finally
You number yourself in the tally
You make a perfect total with your
Aye, rarely said But I have heard you say

Let's stay or you said go
Someone running not unusual
To have to go to work at dawn
Glad for the job happily gone
So let them take our places
And not as we did go but stay
An hour completely red not
Reckless though unearthly
Let's stay you were so
Flushed the way a night will
Make you vague and permeable
Nonsense that you or I should be
En route Look someone running
Away and not unhappy to
Let's stay but you said no

Though you complain about your bruises
Among cushions even here even you might find
Some edge to fall apparently against my will
Though not everything is as soft as I am
And not every impulse toward sympathy
Needed or received or not each attempt
To fit a plug into the wall doesn't explode
In your hand and wounds will come
Though you can hide them well enough
You complain meaning I do since it was
You said that though no one else heard
Nothing can be proved but for those bruises
Which even as you complain are both
More and less than you deserve to have and
Though you have them now are fading

Why am I divided from him?
A continuous line begins with the brow
And becomes the nose by agreement
A piece of linen simplifies
The features of its women like
Masks or any other kind of quiet
A beautiful arrangement by convention
Only if accepted or if not
Why am I divided thoughtlessly?
A stylized head bisecting two scenes
Of life or its embroidered equivalent
House man clouds a child suspended from
Parentheses that by balancing unite and yet
Why am I silent in the foreground divided?

He takes off each shoe with the grace
You sometimes find in drunks ones who
Dress well despite lapses in time
Giving out with a frequency that would be
Alarming if heard or if heard understood
He favors a discrete red and allows
For repetitions in a scarf or even picks up
The theme in trousers or an extravagantly
Open-throated knot as if we could see his heart
He takes off his coat drops and retrieves it
With the elegance of a single move full
Of intent just to show off the deftness
He possesses with a surprising fervor
As you do when it's what or all
You have left or so they'll say when
He takes off but then I'll always see him

And to brave clearness I'd have given
Almost what I did give Nothing
That wasn't strictly speaking mine
Wanting only what was blatant
Giving into the available restraints
With the same passion I might
Have resisted or perhaps I did
For it was the same damn thing
And too brave or too grand for anything
Like what I should have done or been
All things reduced to the absence of these
Same things They rush me to return
On time or even before I've gone and said
Here is to all we are not lamenting
And to brave clearness or to what we have instead

So then as I say I begin again
These days it's always four a.m.
Before I drop off the night's morning
Almost and almost dusk and time
To begin again and again I've missed
The morning approached wrong-
Endedly but then if one end is more
What you want to do then do so
So then offering itself begins with
And remains awake tilted up until
Blood runs to the eyes and it's time to consider
How like any of our mornings is this dusk
The beginning and how I began to say
I begin again exactly as when before claiming
So then as I say I begin I began again

Which thinks only of itself
As a naked woman writing a book
She is in love with you
My mistress he said to me
The same flowers which grew then
We write at random
We go to bed in the sun
What we know to be true
Which thinks only of itself
Or he of herself like dominoes
She spills over into you
He is me
A version of anyone
We write it for them
Which thinks only of itself
A fully grown woman
I am in love with you
She writes everything down
Arguably
We write it out

Before it disappears the implication is strengthened
We are our own audience
I am forced to move in a certain way
By the other members though this place is familiar to me
They are strange transforming everything as they
Go loudly not deciding to I also go
We excite each other
By our multiple presences swelling the parade pushing
Before it this emptiness tends
To disperse in circumstances which
Close in as when cops with sticks
And masks worry the lingering coherence
Of potential events we submit to them
Yet our complicity meaning to have itself lays open
Before it the spectacle of our dissemination

On the borders were prophetesses and scenes
Of liftings one by the other
And climbings effective and not of barred doors
And pilings of groups on roofs of any
Description being stacked too near to see
The progression and its counter filing
Oppositely as much of a sight as if
The intended might have been going on
On the borders inasmuch as the borders
As urgent as the center seemed
To order the disarranged elements
Repeatedly fixing and loosing
The attentions grown expectantly
Keen of their advantage
On the borders finding the complex sufficient

LAURA DE SADE

"To wear binding like binding" she wrote
Also "my name as the title shows
Is Laura" a common enough situation
To be bound as oneself to admit
To unpardonable pride or unusual
Desires "to court sensuosity as if it were
The judge of truth" as its own renouncing
Stands against men in the old sense
To wear down in the arena
Of full view the libertine regalia
Imagined upon a rigorous silence
As when turning back to a woman
Entangled in leaves an animate
Becomes a sentient piercing willfully
"To where a man's heart beating ..."

Chandeliers were existing but I
Decide to say goodbye to my flesh
Apricot walls with what was left
Of the days
Extrapolated
As they already were from the decadence
Of calendars or gardens, fountains
Made to display
The divisible symmetrically
Chandeliers depend upon
The pendulous fullness of someone's bride
The fact of linens fastened with ribbons
To fat beds
That celebrate being stuffed like
Chandeliers we use up the light

The year forces itself out of me
Much as the remaining days
Drain unmercifully the resources each measure
A full measure takes just that much
As can be born by the taker
Whose confession starts a new life
Whose time is identical with
The year we are having
Though we can't have it
The name of the present is determined
By its numbers as if naturally
Because I do the year seems to exist
Consecutively because I lose the count
Doesn't fail to encompass me in
The year's reckoning

Where into the floor were drawn
Fishes and other saleable creatures
Assembled into a flatness
Whose plan enhances
The singularity of each tile
Along with the overall drawing
Of coins from passersby
Making purposefully for stalls
Where in bins the catch
Oiled and made to shine like
Whatever would be freshest
And desirable as the instant
Of perception unites the impulse
To spend with the seller's intuition of
Where she can get her best price

By ending on Saturday the thirteen
Hours and minutes to be determined
By season that interval
Of light in which we find ourselves
Like any other burning complete
With unalterable change
The sameness of ending blackly
By ending on Saturday
There might have been a Golden Age
A bursting treasury
Or only a name
To end it though
By ending here we've ended nothing

Last winter in Florence
A costume drama in progress he writes
Strangely narrow yet embracing
I described him noting suddenly
What my handwriting as an old woman
Will be he continues I am that now
Inside devising a man or woman
Who is manly outside
Last winter fingertips barely
On the street one overcome one
Twisting inside made for the purpose a cloak
Or other garment against time against
The body they were the same constructing
These memoirs out of nothing
Last winter sending them back to me

THE ENTHUSIAST

I am the King's whore. There is writing on a body spread out under itself blatantly at ease. A huge pillow is realistically given. The pillow is part of the imagined context as are the trees of the park. The yellow sky makes a triangle with the red and blue satin of the robe which falls away. The child is mythological. The large ivory jar in the corner is tufted and fluted in three places and knobbed on the top. A fit jar for a King whose fine lines find consonance with the artful brows and hair of the creature before us. Does she intend to be understood in collaboration with her maker?

These verses were written He was with his patroness The present is close to the original Form being imposed From inside the outside looked the same He depicted the relations between them Women pots and trees His hand his mind These were part of a sacred service They didn't call it religion At the end of the century artists embrace their sovereign The bottom is a baroque form The women of that race Their form and his mind and These verses

How to represent water was one of the questions they were unable to imagine How many dimensions does a word have? She occupies a place occupied by Goddesses and Queens because she is an open secret. The King is here because he came back. What became reinstated was his ability to negotiate with his minions. They have no dimentionality either. The fountain appeared in the middle as an image of plenty. The water appeared as light.

That our desire is increased by difficulty was a tender application

And languished in the circle of his arms Among birds her lover The centuries old lawn laid out like an award Should you be willing We will complete the picture Of the arrows she complained Of the ivy crawling up the walls

He grew horns on his forehead by the power of the imagination We bring ourselves back to the form The effect upon the man of his beliefs and estate were thought to be less than we now conceive them to be yet more than could be controlled At the request of His Majesty she lay back picturing a woman like herself A movable icon represented every possible window and door Honeycombed with doubt

The Lady paints a picture A blood red fleur-de-lis extends itself behind her canvas into the same shape in violet There are creases in the material to show its substance She creates this voluminous curtain A marble of a young man whose cloth swathed across his genitals she indicates with a sweeping gesture (He turns toward her) By her seriousness White rolls of paint are made to seem like fur There is a ruling pattern which sticks to her for she is also the model Men with hands above their heads are shouting or falling

"I have this tremendous amount of story" An artist makes a catalogue of exchanges She expresses her concern The King's milk The white collection of blank pages She invests her statement with the enthusiasm she is famous for She will say

I am the King's whore Miss O'Murphy's braid twisted like a halo Dimpled shoulders Around my heart like a cave Another turning The thing she planned to do I wish to stay Tyrranick Love My troubled hours She began I wish to go

These verses appear to say they won't But they are willing She thinks and speaks of herself as separate From the forms of her employment But she is familiar with the continuum The mystic double body of the King The false contract A display of citizenship She thinks of herself as a man possessed These verses argue actual practice Conspicuous gallantry Dear Sir Please accept the threat of

27

my existence As the heart you imagine me to have These verses are not a contradiction

How to represent clarity with a viscous medium by adding color Not personal Not troublesome The emeralds did not keep her chaste She used her gifts to create rules of decorum She could have supported a hundred men with her jewelry If tongue be a woman's arms, how dare you imagine any other kind of soldier

That our desire is increased by use An inspirational logic took over Overspilling in fact like the white breasts that were the fashion The shot silk The tender weapons of his august person They stood in a row like rooms off the hall that he owned Everything was made of stone

And languished stability itself which is nothing more than a languid motion The curling iron gate He opened her mouth to kiss He found all manner of activity going on Inside her head The way he talked The metal which characterized the time

When everyone gets to be King and speak this beautiful language The new knowledge will enable them to impress themselves On nature the private subject imposes itself as a function of the willing Monarch They were of an age The child King The child Bride

I am the King's whore I am a singular desire A trophy An adventuress In the sense of withering away The wager was lost as it was made When light drew itself over her visible body it was a symmetrical feast Lasting into the night There was a black garden rendered by her with an overlaying so that the pigment was an independent skin which threatened to pull away from the picture plane

These verses make appear possible What is this speech today I will have gotten through She tells herself Alive inaccurately He puts a veil over his voice He has taught me his language And I him mine These verses equally unstable Recognize themselves In the broken running taught to soldiers Inventing the lesson as they go along Later seems to them like nature Finds a way to save herself

These verses she says Save yourself

How to represent the theatricality of her love The hot lights tangible with color She made them look that way He filled her lap with pearls

That our desire is increased steadily to the sandy bottom Cool under the structures provided by subjects Vigilant of the pleasures they believe us to be capable Of great exertion On our behalf They never use the word They refer to time as eternity

And languished in the circle of his arms

THE ORAL TRADITION

interpretation. They
The broadness of her smile
At low tide the many
A well-proportioned room
Escaping creatures
How will they survive
Being correct
Being swallowed in fact the correct
interpretation. They
Where attached to other versions
Of themselves a sustenance
Of course they don't survive
The initial entwining
Though being the same is itself
interpretation. They

singular. Caught
As they are in an extended
Association of something like
Place or plate
Imagine everything most profligate
In dancing and sitting down together
The taking of meat
A man by a woman
Singular but general
As eating is organized
This is like eating
That drawn from himself
One must go out
And not remain though remaining
singular. Caught

by the air necessarily upborne
If you can renew any impulse upon it
Faster than the air can recede
From the pressure
You cannot fail to keep it up
"And this is a good, a true thing, perpendicular to the
          ground
Like the freshest, least complicated and earliest of
          memories"
You are cradled
by the air or by the softer ground
In the utopia of continuing
The return is effortless
Stopping included even
Something direct - the rending of a fuselage
by the air fails

to allow for the fall by now
Seen as inevitable
In the distance California
Black and blue formations
He or she upside down
Incessantly wet on the coast
The noise of the approach camouflaged
to allow us though invisible
To consume space
The world ends
With a gray area
The ocean is predictable
But we have gone out of our way
to allow for the powerful

need to be more than equal. Each
The finish is thick and lusterless
The intonation like a day late in August
Or like the real Augustans
The landed ones
"I do a lot of traveling with my voice"
At this angle the ocean
Or anything else is permeable
Need is overwhelmed by plenty
Each submergence like the future
We are here provisionally
But it makes you hard
The need to eat changes meaning
What part of the head
needs the mouth. Or what counts

The range of stations spanned
In my search for three four time among
The stridencies which commonly
And barely divide the noise from
The noise outside preferred often even
Machines have a key neighbors their
Sing song argument windowed halls
Open to eyes and the sun and not
Unlike the country homes and waltzes of
The range beyond whose blank rolling
Close the woods where my lover's husband
Has built a house for his children and
She and the mud and white squares
Of music the wood blackens with age and opens out
The range vibrates to where the senses stop

LA MALINCHE

Money was anything that came to hand

She had lips for his eyes

(a violent forgetting that forced return)

Because there was no electricity

A man fucked

Because there was no water

A woman from behind

The children passed into the train

She was spent

The iron money of the Spartans

We wished we were already there.

Pressed between them

Black inside the train. The landscape was red. In the dark
sacristy the heavy lace and peculiar smell of holy water.

The green cross of the Inquisition set into the local pink stone.

The circulation of money

The water was infused with a way of life

Or buried

Yes I know it the Tacuba. Green and black light. Pink and green frosting like stone.

The one you don't want to lose

"Of the Series of Masked Aggressions"

Black tea with heated cream in copper.

Or blending with the street where

The lions. Blue tiles. The House of the Inquisitor has balconies which fly over the street.

As official interpreter she put his orders in the form of rhetorical suggestions tinged with irony.

He put himself inside her mind

Surrounded by souls. A hundred men in black and silver costumes play as they scream.

She had lips painted gold

On the day of the burning everything was draped in green.

Charged with being enlightened.

They close around him

The dark air of the city. She was forbidden to come. There is always a red zone. It means nothing.

Even if "understanding" here means "destroying"

The sound of *geodas*

A white flowered pitcher sells itself. The weaving machine in the hotel Goya. The carriage carries us through the trouble which is black and blue.

Were thighs made unstable

Those who take on the manners of foreigners.

Because beaten or flattered

The Annunciation here retitled Temptation of the Virgin.

He would do.

The twisted train on its back. Corn spills out. A dark woman in her best dress is transparent.

These romantic landscapes also contain elements of desire, skepticism and anguish.

We found them buried in the remains of the river.

They called him by her name.

From inside a shudder

But coins were not the first money.

The monkey put

We meet again for ices. The color is poison.

"Cortez's Henchmen Contemplating the Demons of the New World"

The dead people at the edge of town. The play in the language of the conquerors.

A Saint signed by the Treasurer. Every day there was new money.

Because there was no water

She took it

There were no equivalents

The glass coins of Egypt, the knife money of China

She had enough

She had lips for his eyes
A man fucked
A woman from behind
Pressed between them
Or buried
The one you don't want to lose
Or blending on the street where
He put himself inside her mind
She had lips painted gold
They close around him
Were thighs made unstable
Because beaten or flattered
From inside a shudder
She took it
She had enough

CUENCA

Someone real dies
Being reminded of dying

The crowd gave way around them cheering. Children marched. She spoke in two languages. There were echoes and distortion. Two clowns represented the government. The word for eye in her language was like the word for gold.

As I imagine her she is already gone. She had a place in mind. She went back to the other world. That night I saw her again in a report. She spoke as if of the future. Her features were indistinct. They were in a square in the corner. Heads filled the picture. I couldn't recognize myself. I could have been anybody.

We see her through screens and lenses flattened out and framed importantly as if in gold. Things said so often in the context of one language as to become empty in the context of another. I couldn't see her. Felt numb. Saw nothing. Every few seconds the picture changed.

I realize how little I know

She describes her home. It's like a wooden bowl. It's hot in the valley. That spring we came across. The bodies out of the river. The movement. You can see in this portrait behind my head indistinctly but it's really green and clear. I was a writer in that language.

Or alternately I am not that one
Going mindlessly forward

Wearing a flower in her chest she spoke to the assembly. Later in the makeshift hospital. There are records. There are sheets taped to the walls. As if bronze were poured onto the whole topography including the rising and falling of voices later not included. There was a stiffening of waves into historically familiar patterns. Her culture also uses the rose in this way.

There is no private life. She looked back at me with that oddly televised stare. Her name for the last set of notes. The radio was powerful. The other radio came in under it. One can often hear her on the local station. There is continuity. There is an absence of rhetorical pathos.

> But does how you go
> Matter is what you become

A badge or name card or something else written appeared to peel back. The script was a personal one. A second image as of a repeated portrait occurred as a fault of reception. That was the memory of the first meditation on what was to become the event. Perhaps it was at the same time. We imagine such things. The infectious power of a sequence including what was not planned. I thought it was torture to see her that way.

Her dress and hair stand out against the gold. An entire room is pictured. I had imagined someone. She was that person. At places the light made the gold look silver. The black was static. What was going to happen had already happened.

The crowd gave up, putting its head in its hands. They lost their identity as a crowd. They were each identifiable. Others were in love. Crowds can love. Perhaps it was only crowd love as when a desirable woman like an old painting represents a country dying in its ruins.

40

            The picture they have of you
            Someone real caught

So that later in its houses before its televisions the crowd could still
be seen in thought as well as mechanically. We were also
described in words. And by the same time on another day when
we had ceased to exist there was another in a long line of deaths.
She made a beautiful report.

There is a portrait in a broken gold frame. Glass or plastic is held
in front by tape. It seems makeshift. It is a reproduction. The face
is indistinct. There are two faces. Paper or gauze or a fine plastic
mesh sticks to the face in layers. The ink is smeared. The process
stopped somewhere in the middle. It seems to continue. The
portrait doesn't reach to the edge of the frame. The flower can be
seen clearly near the bottom between her dress and her chest.

            Without a time or place
            Decisions unmade plans
            Being taken so completely

Your own voice played back approaches the effect of the
remembered speech of someone absent. Questions are asked by
rote as in a catechism. The responses from another catechism
change the tone which can then be heard as wanton or militaristic.
The children got through by chance. They were stunned by the
attention. I wondered how to interpret her constant cheerfulness.

            This has been called dancing

Equally absent I am interviewed in a dream. I know this writer.
The questions are a source of control. We accede to it gladly. We
react. The public facts are these.

41

There aren't any children in the next version. They weren't really like children. The event or act was given as if she were present. We knew her so badly we are mistaken in imagining who is left. The new person reads a list of similar demonstrations.

> But we are the same
> Someone real gets older

The crowd opens up before her simultaneously mute. Seeing is entering. We believed it. The contents are sustaining but unavailable. Having invented a character we miss her as she smiles back at us without a body except by inference. I am not here. We endow her with everything she doesn't have. We include life.

I fall into the negative ecstasy of the radio
Waves around me now immediacy
Has its chance even occasionally in concert
With the surrounding songs I locate
Continuing however imperceptibly to change
The sense lifted wholesale from the air
Amplified by infinite reception
I drink myself to death in my rocking chair
I know everything now
The feminine counterpart of the fool is justice
Compromised my belief in entertaining
This collaboration in effect a state
Of fascination and vertigo whose
Waves I am insensible to information increasingly
I can conceive of total control

Tender lineaments were becoming the lines of his face having arrived in paradise that round look loosening as it did the accustomed tightness of his eyes contributing even to a slackness that he believed was good, natural and caused by himself. Everything was useful here.

The horizon formed of newsprint was in a direct line with the focus of his usual contemplation. There was a woman drawn to seem both clothed and naked. Stuck there were torn edges of pictures from brochures, children's books and letters. One letter in particular suggested a certain intimacy. It was impossible to read "Though I've made love with her" was the longest phrase that was legible. The rest was torn or drawn over. The writing was not presented so as to satisfy one's curiosity about it, but only as another line to lead the eye around the work. Knowing the artist, he knew the story, or thought he did, or could at least picture the woman whose steady hand had been incorporated here into the design.

Florence

A reader at a round table. She recalls a picture of a woman sleeping at a table next to an open door. An artist dreams of another more terrifying threshold. She writes of it. They both read and talk about it. Later she reads dreamily remembering their talk.

The element of idealization was present to an extent that obscured the individuality of her features which were too strong. She wore symmetrical folded things was short-haired, pale almost to grayness. She was difficult to follow and took up a large amount of space which she seemed to be constantly backing out of.

This verism, pageantry, balance and restraint all contributed to a sustained, contemplative mood that could be described as implied action in introspective repose.

He looked like the devil to his designer with whom he had, as he believed, collaborated on the creation of what they referred to as his space. Suspended in an upward curve of the building, the suite extended airily out into what seemed from below an oddly effeminate balcony. There were many apparently soft surfaces to charm one kind of client and make another feel unsure. On the only people who interested him it had no effect at all. The girl for instance scorned its purchased arrangement, valuing only any order demonstrative of a lack of respect for manmade laws. The presence of money undermined these fondly held values however, lending a gaiety to her demeanor not often otherwise found. The designer, he had noticed, also grew fuller and stronger with each considered expenditure, each precious subtlety. Money was simply the medium in which he worked.

The exotic had often made its way into his compositions. Nationality, internationality, was of interest. National character seemed at times to him to exist, its effects to be capable of being calculated and exploited. There were cuttings from the portfolio he had made when he went back. He put them in, took them out again. There were a few pictures of nudes, women half-submerged in the inland sea which had so occupied his attention at that time. These were difficult to account for. Finally with a sense of the correctness of this perversion, he kept them in. A kind of frenetic pencilling came close again to blocking them out, did actually obscure a part of one figure.

My lover's name was a refrain she allowed herself. It had a foreign quality. She toyed with the letters, wrote, considered, shortened and lengthened it. A difficult thing to have the name of a man or, as she herself, of a city, and, in this furthest instance, of a conqueror. They had once made something of that.

She had the authority of a massive head of hair. Framing her speech, even when wound in a knot, the potential existed for its dark weight to fall around, in this case, her interlocutress. That amount of hair little moved by a toss of the head and she, not given to unconscious movements, would sweep it up holding herself in such a way that the expressions she encountered in conversation were often vacant or troubled. There was a kind of taking both in her aggressive occupation of the area between them and in the negative space left by her narrow impossibly arched position.

The Ocean City complex was an unusual meeting place. The use of chrome and glass, tiles and cursive neon argued a timeliness that was both monumental and tawdry, merely modern, impossible to maintain because made of questionable materials. It was like a ruin of the future - peeling, cracked even as the workmen were replaced by the first crowds. Today there remained potted plants covered with red satin ribbons like awards. Searching the purple carpeted steps she seemed to see her lover looming somewhat awkwardly large among young Chinese men and women. She would resemble some of the girls whose willowly mannequin-like sense of costume she shared, and had also now in common with them that she was from or going to somewhere else, not reachable or present.

Alexandria

Disarranged by the winds gathered at the foot of the largest buildings she regarded them. The vaguely Greek remains of one had been emptied and attached to a modern tower. The floor was glossy, as was the black fountain. The air was wet. Taken up by the wind her hair and what could have been called her gown became increasingly disordered. She seemed to be waiting patiently but was completely lost. The addition of an angular blond man to her side attracted some attention probably because they were almost inimically different. He seemed to cancel her out, though she was no less present for being cancelled. Her power was not dependent on assertion but on a sort of pervasiveness, as if film coated or filtered everything. At first he was relieved to find her, then apparently irritated or angry perhaps at the stiffness of her embrace or her obliviousness to being late and out of place. However, she reacted with real emotion to what she perceived to be the new watch strapped to his wrist. She bent extravagantly over it causing him, by an abrupt movement, to pull her inside the building (which, in a sense, he owned) thereby ending the public part of their conversation.

The background of the collage was done in a way that evoked a manner of painting redolent of what was thought to have suggested in the past the human touch. He had known that this approach was impossible at the same time he was becoming obsessed with its implications. That it was taboo and therefore desirable and inevitably his particular future, he was aware. But giving in could never happen, might never occur until it was exactly overwhelming. The almost physical presence of his engagement was as unquestionable as it was intermittant. He never stopped resisting and there was satisfaction in going either way.

This letter we are forming Made of your front to my back Though familiar as the alphabet May be made strange by emphasis As the fact of numerical equivalents In some languages letters and numbers and In our language the possible entrances To be grandly made This letter will open up a lot of doors For you my dear I said quoting Our mutual friend invoking the tale Freshly told of our last encounter She does this to me I demonstrated Having made my confession to her but to you I offer This letter we are together forming

Her understanding was restful to him except when it was intrusive or completely unsettling. Their places were a series of platforms, portrayals of what they believed was going on. There were constant negotiations as at borders which existed physically and otherwise in the home which they constructed, taking it simultaneously back down, around them.

Because the girl was permeable each of them would suddenly find themselves in the invigorating environment of her lack of will. She laughed it off. He was giddy, trembling and hard. Each undressing revealed more of her than he expected. She seemed so slight in her clothes that her breasts, for instance, were surprisingly fat, her hair thicker, blacker. She, for her part, was appreciative of a certain perfection she believed him to possess of something that had melted down and crystalized again. Sometimes his attention wandered as if he were unwilling to localize his passion, to put a beginning and end to it. At these times she worked on him until, as she saw, he was really smiling.

The impossibility finally of owning anything began to oppress him. His desire to apply personal, domestic values to his business made him look there for a sense of security and completion rarely found anywhere and least of all in his particular enterprise. The language, the fact, of getting in and getting out suggested that these were actually places to be. He felt himself surrounded by his own plans which had taken the form of well designed but completely empty space.

Queasy from heights and fatigue, the building, at this crest of itself, wound visibly around her. Having sex with another human being in a elevator was, as much as anything, what she liked having and therefore, at times, getting beyond. The figures she was now able to manipulate were attaching themselves to increasingly larger entities. She experienced the situation as of being taken up by numerous sequences, the end of oneself or the beginning of something else, representing the merest extra turn in only one of them.

Book two begins here
They become citizens
Able to notice the quality
Of anywhere that it has no
Limit to the world
That becomes so many words
The more for my not having said
Of them that believing as they do no
Book or belief resolves into
That sort of beginning again that
Sort cannot be depended upon
To initiate the already well worn
Sight in the sense of place clearly
Able to be had or seen to open as that
Book too seems to begin here

In the new environment in real time
The question of material means
The actor carries his piece of the city
Of facades and columns, faces
A hand holding a letter
Without intonation, without length
Squandering words and money
There is no accumulation of time
In the new meaning acquired by common
Phrases like we don't all come from there
But are made to seem the same by longing
As a way to engender a situation
The eager sacrifice of our more complex
Rhythmic needs to putting down this form
In the new version we give it all away

We here become citizens
The ordinary quality of the sun
Makes our day indistinguishable
From what you see to what you want
To see exaggerated as a decision
The appearance of which was among
Our rights the only inviolable
Illusions preserved by our constitution
We here appeal to you as if you
Framed by the force of your caption
Were able to make those determinations
We now know are made on the basis
Like a street in the middle of nowhere
Of interest because it is present
We here see nothing beyond our control

Fitting this shot against one including
The uncontrollable desires of others
Through any degree of distortion
Or of oneself for the material
The speech without response they speak of
Luckily not us we think in unison
Starting again they don't count
The transparency assumed between us
Fitting against itself with a consciousness
Of being live which is more than life
Allowed to go unspoken indefinitely
As now the mouth seems to form
Around the stuff given then taken up
But less than what was actually swallowed
Fitting as it does against the heart

All we wanted
A chart of interruption
To go back
Paying the check in another life
Is shortened to pain
We return as each other
An orphan an unmarked craving
For the drink we forget in his honor
All we wanted to go on
Saying he is history
We mean business
The equivalent of the play
Is the body speaking back at us
The physical parting
All we wanted

Asking not to be read he wears
An unexamined mask
One of us
Reddened like an animal with lips
He gambles ass backwards
Because he is legible
They are my lips
We are attached to him
Asking not to be spared
The thickening that comes
With age and desire
Spread over his face
We read what he watches
Asking us not to stop

Belief in the planetary day
In this calendar the sense
Firm as with a man
That a body is on top of you
Marching along
Your diary is red and fat
You keep track of your love
With figures enacting midsong
Belief in a revolving position
Organized into a woman
We get her slowly
We are in time
The constellations in an orgy
Above as below
Belief is all over

There's not much left of the moon
It's snowing in the capital

Or it's too cold to snow

There's not much left of a pond
By definition the moon in the moon's arms
Warns that what will happen

Frozen in the center
As if knowing the future
There's not much left of the moon

Is the city visible
Now that it's almost night
But not as dark
A mountain from here
As pale as winter
I couldn't breathe
The bed was like snow
Now that it's clearing
Is the city with us
Again away
To see everything
I uncover myself as proof
Against existing
All night from a distance
Is the city the same

Each thing she watches
Exaggerates someone pretends
That the moon is as big as the water
Or that it makes a difference
Which of us is the girl
Drowning is another way to say
The excuses are ended
That rose from her desire
Each thing she watches
Has become double
Inside and white like a black day
Inaccessible from this place
Each thing she watches

What am I
Aloud is the answer
To what do I want
As a question or as
A woman for example
One might be asked
Which is like repetition
What can be asked of me or you or
What can I
Be allowed to know or
To act as if existing conditions
Have made me exist
For you saying say what I want
Here name finally mine is
What I want

Of you as a word
Refers outward to the world
Or in to pleasure
Are you equal to
The present includes possibility
Only if addressed
You have sent me a letter or not
Or I have not the wherewithall to speak
Of you to you
As if you were a plan
A construct enterable
Or only terrible like dreams
Of you without you in them
Do they have to do with anything
Of you as you are there

In that place
An arrangement being made
In an imagination not unlike
Mine might be formal
A real deal in which things
Are signed vows taken
I take them to mean
What they have now
Said about imagining
In that place where
I am now imaginary as you
Being not but in thought
Here though here you are a question
Who you are being another
In that place

Undefined momentarily
Empty unknown even by one
Who should know as yourself
Or I should but don't
As if knowledge like complicity
Beside itself incapable
Because only we can know
In that sense
Undefined as we
Only a word easily used
To mean both
What it means and what
It could mean much
More than it does
Undefined as it is

As is implies risk
To the buyer in this case
Let's say I or you
Having as little as we have had
Of each other or time
Value equals time given
And what taken
Let's say I have taken you
As is or you me
Is suggestive
But we know empty
Meaning not to have but so far
Not meaning nothing
Implies to take
As is something

This is something
We have arrived
The future is behind us
But there is no one here or one
Literal all the time
Could refer to anyone
But refers to you
Who no longer know what
This is or who
You are a delight to me now
In your bliss wedded as I am
To the present I give
I am at home
But writing in a wind storm
This to you

NORMANDIE

The old world has to say
Lane of trees brick blue or slate
Gulls sparrows crows
Whatever you want if you
Pay is the absence of the apple
The judgment of Paris
Always a mistake
The old way is like this
Here are the fruits
A woman makes her lover hard
They both look at him
Of the sea displaced
The black shells lay discarded
The old offer

My ears do a fan dance
A woman practices a routine
On a dark stage the light
Flat against tits a twisted
Cord around also
Hips also pale and listens
To direction the exchange
Of dinner and striptease
My ears are yours is like
The end of the dance
Less apparent than open innocently
She is winning you say
You have my eyes or you have
My ears meaning the other sense of going into

Crushing the fruit into the drink
They say the sea is different here
As the coast is skewed
The waves come in from the side
The sun sets anywhere
The rocks they say
Holding their skirts above their knees
Step out into the sea
Crushing themselves into pebbles
The birds are drunk again
Speaking their own language
Always abrupt say each
Other each other
Crushing everything in their mouths

Who could I be wondering
That she at my table
In black a pale
Older perhaps
Though not close to
Invasion day was
Years ago at least
No one remembers
Who could tell the story
People come to rest here
Or were liberated and built
This invisible wall that
Warms without burning
A child pretends to laugh
More peaceful than I
Who could not allow the extra

The last one at the cafe
Has no sense of time or date
Or obligation but thinks
Of longing almost
Face an intake of breath
There is a start or
Hesitation as if saying can I
Yes this person yourself
The last one plus one
As a gull drops and then snaps
Back up the thing it wants
To believe existing leave
A tip for the country drinks
The creatures from the sea
Left but for
The last one

But you (What pleasure you
Make sounds you don't
Only I do also
Here not with but
With the present perfect
Could you this
Or can not
But do admit
That you know
What pleasure I
Knew or in the present
Or now soon
What done or would or will
If these are only always of love or of
What pleasures you) know

THE BAROQUE POEMS

Invocation (as if to Mercury)

I know who you are
Where you live
When you were a child
There was no time There is no time
Like the present

You are mine
I am made to say these things
As if we were in a play or game
And these were moves

Or lines supple and nervous
And your eyes
And I

Yours in the sense of captured
As in love or as in that was not a game

And this is not the prize

Oracle

When we

Use the same words
Hold them to your head
Like a shell of itself
But picture the thing
Painted red

Like insects crushed into chemicals
Their bodies into drugs
Without feeling impossible or inappropriate
They include everything

Details of heroes and divinities
But it's the short version
And the movement continues

Beyond the music so you are left
Moving to nothing

Or the same thing

highe Helen

Although not archt
Though not of gold

She is my Helen
   (Someone claims falsely)
At the Gate

"No lust there's like to poetry."

One Act

We risk
Hesitation
You touch a hot thing
And say is it possible
To keep on burning

Could I have said that
His invented figure
Becomes her real character
But they don't look the same

Look at her eyes
She doesn't have any
Then in this plain style

This thus should she says
Be included (or turned away)

"highe Helen, the fair"

2 versions

One virgin to another
I think of evil
In front of people
I disappear
An oath

Between us
This not existing
Is not as hard as it looks
But the distance

Dissolved also
As if in a waltz
I saw her beauty

Unselfconsciously
I stopped thinking

As a virgin

Your first woman

In the manuscript version

Mettle, vigor, strength

Crown of thorns vase

Or the same Medusa. Red rocks inside a glass jar. Metallic
snakes.

Ask her.

A vow to Mars

Metal touches metal
It was frightening
Of all the raging Waves
Into a froth
So soon again still inside

He pours water
On my head
Some gets in my eyes
Some gets in my mouth

Mouth
The house
The secret room

The picture consistent
Or inconsistent but imaginary

And the room

Her complaint

She tells me everything
As plain as this
And I say it's up to you
Only I don't say it
But find

The half-moon is up
Before falling back
To the surface
Let me take you

Or be taken
The waterless seas
Called the maria

Another name
For your virtue

Is mine

In your robe

Sex imagined
The cult of Venus
Like a Babylonian freeway
Or a videotape of clouds
All electrons

The wind moves things around
A jet trail also
Disheveled An owl or pheasant
Bursts from woods In the city

We do what we want
My favorite part of you
The white temple

Is behind the woman
In this picture

Of Helen

Like a halo

About her flesh
She paints it on
Her body as plain as metal
She says
One other time

I said this praise
And didn't lie either
Then
Or now (or not yet)

Equally
I write the words to her song
Which say now

In as many ways as we can
In as short a time

As we have

One

Here was a startling picture: a red-hot planet
wrapped in clouds of ice!

No moon

Another

And again
Another day
Another time
Another

All start with you

Feast of the Annunciation

A drunk nun pouring over her book of hours. Drunk with grace. The Black Hours of Charles the Rash. The script known as bastarda. As if someone were looking over her shoulder.

The color changed the pages into a kind of glass

Her hat like a steeple

The rash hours

The world green like an apple

The annuciation

The animal in her lap

Little Egypt

The "sweet" project
I know you keep dream diaries
But your esthetic proclivities
As open tonight
As we are

The feeling of form without
Sensation of volume
Is what is wanted
Is not what is wanted

The fluid boundary
The aftermath
Of moving between

Exactly!
"Afectos varios de su corazón"

(The various affects of the heart, the movement)

Between sexes

Mercury

How she got her strength
Like a sheperdess
Is naked
Like a lost summer
Creature though it's winter now

He is a she
We are in a partnership
Alone
With one of them

Pale as snow
He calls to me
Expect nothing

This is not a trick
You are not a woman

Like I am

New Year's Eve

Without anxious scrutiny
We call ourselves
What we choose
Knowing innocence
Not to be

The promised landscape
She strides seems real
Stuffed with beeswax
Lime, hemlock, lead

Enough to reveal danger
The Babe that (like a Bride)
Or from another perspective

A pyramid of plaster cast brains
A pile of black cats

Whether or not

Feast of the Epiphany

We look it up
Though no copy is known
Highly polished
When I see
Looking back from the sky

Like trussing in falconry
One who prays for a benefactor
Mercury for example
Or something else metallic

The words I said
Come back for more
Meet the others in my head

My reflection
"Mercury that boy has given me back

my strength"

Three creatures

All birds

Five lines for Helen

They read no
Ownership

Worthless bad

Another

Of the person bewitched by her

A treatise of the passions and faculties

His secret will
Performed
Is available
Even to one who pretends
To resist

Speak for yourself
I tell myself
But his blankness
Invading

Gray painted on my hands and arms
Like a dream in which
Nothing stops stops me

Being nothing
Like the new sounds

You have begun to make

Drawing on metal

A fountian sacred to some deity
Has no history
Not useful
(Part of the creame from that Religious Spring)
To us

Sensation flows along the lines
Along the bodies but they
Lines and bodies
Already inhabit the place

Which shows through where metal
And flesh
This rain

All the time
And the blankness (flesh)

Where this line

Night today

More light as if plain
Night today
Black evergreen white Saints
Peter and Paul whiter
Sky

An electronic horizon
Birds made out of atoms
No depth
Beyond the curtains

It's day again
After the rain
All day inside or night

In one place
Plain

That you

Another one

The dream is no
Question the answer
Also no

"Give way and be ye ravisht by the Sun"

Who are you? What do you want?

The moon

overpowers The Sun
never
The clear water puzzles
Likenesse
Liking

Fierce Hot Wisht
Stolen ceremony
Kings and Queens meet
Secret lest in their sight the sinne

Singular meeting sullen
Double the night personified
Has dew Is

new-formed light is not Isis she
resigned but resisting is this

There is no Helen

Strangely

We already are
Undecided
Doesn't begin to describe
Or yes or know
Swiftly me before him drove

What you are about
Helen is alone
In the intermediate night
You and I

Know you know
Time is upon us
Helen is right to be afraid

Something barely exists
In its twilight

Or wakes in anger

Nemesis

The new song
Replaces winter
With dilemma
Without hesitation
Spring is declared

How did we know each other
Limitless
Not that faire field
The city spring

Searches the air
A figure surrounded
When evil flowers

With traditional appeal
A tropical invasion

Unstated

The man in

You standing so
Attention yours
My mouth
The drink of the
Wings folded up

Gods might
Wander
Attention stopped
Envy dancing

The man in my head
As he put it (said)
Almost blanked out

The moon is it
What I wanted I said

It is it was

Of this edition,
26 have been lettered A through Z
and signed by the author.

OTHER ROOF BOOKS

Andrews, Bruce. Getting Ready To Have Been Frightened. 116p. $7.50.
Andrews, Bruce. R & B. 32p. $2.50.
Andrews, Bruce. Wobbling. 96p. $5.
Bee, Susan [Laufer]. The Occurrence of Tune. Text by Charles Bernstein.
  9 plates, 24p. $6.
Benson, Steve. Blue Book. Copub with The Figures. 250p. $12.50.
Bernstein, Charles. Controlling Interests. 88p. $6.
Bernstein, Charles (editor). The Politics of Poetic Form. 246p. $12.95.
Child, Abigail. From Solids. 30p. $3.
Davies, Alan. Active 24 Hours. 100p. $5.
Davies, Alan. Signage. 184p. $11.
Day, Jean. A Young Recruit. 58p. $6.
Dickenson, George-Therese. Transducing. 175p. $7.50.
Di Palma, Ray. Raik. 100p. $9.95.
Dreyer, Lynne. The White Museum. 80p. $6.
Eigner, Larry. Areas Lights Heights. 182p. $12, $22(cloth).
Gottlieb, Michael. Ninety-Six Tears. 88p. $5.
Grenier, Robert. A Day at the Beach. 80p. $6.
Hills, Henry. Making Money. 72p. $7.50. VHS videotape $24.95.
  Book & tape $29.95.
Inman, P. Red Shift. 64p. $6.
Legend. Collaboration by Andrews, Bernstein, DiPalma, McCaffery, and Silliman.
  Copub with L=A=N=G=U=A=G=E. 250p. $12.
Mac Low, Jackson. Representative Works: 1938-1985. 360p. $12.95, $18.95
  (cloth).
McCaffery, Steve. North of Intention. 240p. $12.95.
Perelman, Bob. Face Value. 72p. $6.
Robinson, Kit. Ice Cubes. 96p. $6.
Seaton, Peter. The Son Master. 64p. $4.
Sherry, James. Part Songs. 28p. $10.
Sherry, James. Popular Fiction. 84p. $6.
Silliman, Ron. The Age of Huts. 150p. $10.
Silliman, Ron. The New Sentence. 200p. $10.
Templeton, Fiona. YOU-The City. 150p. $11.95.
Vega, Janine Pommy. Candles Burn in Memory Town. 107 p. $6.
Ward, Diane. Never Without One. 72pp. $5.
Ward, Diane. Relation. 64p. $7.50.
Watten, Barrett. Progress. 122p. $7.50.
Weiner, Hannah. Little Books/Indians. 92p. $4.

For ordering or complete catalog write: SEGUE DISTRIBUTING,
303 EAST 8th STREET, NEW YORK, NEW YORK 10009